*Dedicated to my mother, Linn,
for instilling in me a passion for
books that is insatiable.*

They say that everyone has at least one book in them.

Since you've picked up this book, I'm guessing that you're thinking about writing one yourself. Like any venture, writing a book will be a learning curve for you but one that is exciting and rewarding.

The Book Book is more than just a guide on how to write your own book. You'll learn the basics of custom publishing and how it can benefit you. It's very much a book that you can dip in and out of depending on the stage you're at with your writing.

In this technological age, a book is a perfect marketing tool. A book is timeless and if some thought is put into it to create a beautifully crafted product, it will engage people with a personal touch and the returns to the writer will be more than just financial. It doesn't matter if you write a poetry book or a huge tome on your experiences in finance, each has its own unique appeal.

Think about this: companies pay huge amounts of dollars to advertise on TV for a thirty second commercial. They don't receive direct revenue from that commercial but they build their reputation. A book can do this as well as bring you extra income if you choose to sell it.

A book is an interactive product that entertains, inspires and persuades people, unlike the interruption of ads on TV or online. It's the perfect way to convey ideas, values and messages from yourself to your reader.

It takes, on average, ten to fifteen hours to read a book. What other medium engages someone for that amount of time? It's your chance to 'talk' with a person one to one.

So what might be YOUR reason to write a book?

it would be pretty cool

you have
something to say

build your profile/business

mark a special anniversary

MAKE MONEY

leave a legacy

promote a cause

have fun

share a message

MAKE A
DIFFERENCE

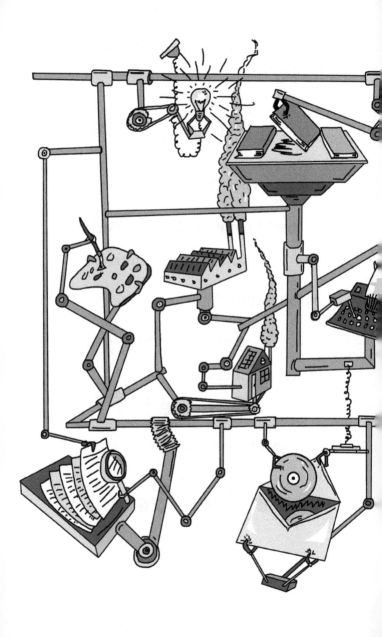

CONTENTS

think

Writing a book is actually a lot of work so I suggest that you do some thinking first to work out the direction that you'll take whilst at the same time working out if it's worth the effort. Sit down and ask yourself some serious questions. The reason for this is that many books fail financially. Why do you think this is? The biggest reason is that there has been no planning.

Writing a book should be tackled like a small business venture. Even if you intend to send it to a traditional publisher, you will have more chance of gaining a contract if you do the hard work for them. This means thinking about who your readership is, the current market and the type of book it'll be.

If you've never written a book before, you may ask yourself, *Who am I to write a book about anything?* If you can answer that, you will have cleared the first big hurdle. For example, if you're writing a how-to book, maybe you have years of experience to share. But how do you know you even have the skill to write it? There are many ways to improve your writing skills but if you find that you don't have what it takes, maybe you can consider a ghostwriter.

The next question is, *How do you know there is a market for your book?* This is where a little research is handy. Go onto Google or Amazon and see if there are other books available that are similar to your idea. Better yet, go into a bookstore or library and find books on your topic. It might be that you already know there is a gap in the market, which has prompted you to consider writing about it. You'll also need to know if you have enough material to fill a whole book.

So what's your big idea?

Once you have the seed of an idea you can begin to formulate your book into something concrete. Quite often a story is born from a simple question like, *How would a child feel if she was conceived purely to be a donor for her ill sister?* What about the simple idea of a cookbook full of recipes that only need four ingredients (a fantastic idea that was rejected by traditional publishers but made the creators rich and famous when they self-published).

The Book Book – the idea

I'm in the business of publishing and I especially love helping people custom publish – a very rewarding exercise. I know I have writing skills because I'm already in the industry and have years of experience. I also know that there is more than enough material to fill a book. In fact, because I wanted a pocketbook format, I had to think about what to leave out, without diluting the material.

Write your idea(s) here:

choose

When you walk in to a book store or the library, you'll see thousands of books. It's really important to have some idea of what you think your finished book might look like. Will it be a big glossy coffee table book or a simple little poetry collection? Don't forget that you also have the option of creating an ebook, which is much less expensive than a printed book in terms of production. The options are endless. You can publish any kind of book you desire.

You also need to consider what genre your book will be. Do you know how many genres there are? Here are some common ones:

Novel – fiction

There are of course many categories that fit into this genre. Things to consider here are the age of your reader, what type of fiction it is (contemporary, historical maybe science-fiction etc.).

Short story collection

Short stories have had a resurgence over the past few years and they are considered a craft distinct from novels. There are instances where a short story has been made in to a movie, like *Brokeback Mountain.*

Children's book

There are people who set out to write a children's book only to find it much more dificult than they thought but the children's book market is very strong and a worthwhile industry to get into if you can.

Poetry collection

There are many beautiful ways you can showcase your poetry in a collection.

Family history

Is there a significant event happening in your family, like a wedding, a wedding anniversary or a family reunion? A family history can be a fun project for the family and a great legacy.

Memoir

Maybe you've had an interesting life and it's been suggested to you that you should write it down. You can choose to do this as a memoir or an autobiography.

How to – general non-fiction

You could write a book about a topic, like a species of bird that is endangered or the best coffee shops in Melbourne.

How to – your expertise

If you have a hobby or business and you feel you have great skills to share, you could write a book about it. A book can be about anything from beekeeping to breeding snakes to building a business.

Current trends

New technologies or interesting inventions could make you a leader in your field. People will be looking for information on how to get into your field or use that latest technology from Social Media marketing and beyond.

Thought leadership/manifesto

New ideas or old ideas revisited can be very interesting to a reader looking for answers to their own questions. You may have been on your own spiritual journey and sharing that journey can help others.

The Book Book – the choice

I run workshops for people wanting to write a book. It's hard to give all the information that has taken me years to accumulate to someone else in a short space of time. This meant that I had a perfect scenario to put together some basic ideas to help people navigate the book-writing process. Publishing and writing are by no means secret or require special skills. By being armed with a few basics before you start, you will save yourself some time and money while enjoying the process.

I knew I wanted *The Book Book* to be a pocketbook so that the reader isn't overwhelmed with information. It is by no means a comprehensive guide but something to get you started while at the same time arming you with enough information to create the finished book.

What is the story you want to tell?

Once you've decided on the genre, what form will the book be?

+ Novel
+ Journal
+ Letters
+ Poetry
+ Essay
+ Report
+ Commentary
+ Guidebook
+ Coffee-table book

Even if you think that you will try to get a publisher to publish it, it's a good idea to think about the format of your book, especially if you intend to include images, quotes, pull-out boxes etc.

Have a look at books in bookstores or at the library and consider these things:

+ Height
+ Width
+ Word count
+ Number of pages
+ Retail price
+ Soft or hard cover

- Colour or black and white images
- Look of the cover – gloss or matte finish
- Binding – perfect, saddle, staple, burst, spiral
- Type of paper stock.

And if you really want to go all out and make your book a beautiful artistic object you might also like to consider:

- Cover flaps
- A dust jacket
- CD in back cover
- Treatments to the cover like embossing
- Inserts
- Paper stock variations
- A bookmark/ribbon.

Jot down the physical aspects of your book:

Format
_____

Retail price
_____

Cover
_____

Type of paper
_____

Cover finish
_____

Binding
_____

Extras
_____

_____

_____

_____

_____

_____

_____

_____

_____

_____

_____

_____

_____

_____

_____

Who will read your book?

First you need to determine what the purpose of your book is.

The Book Book has the purpose to inform people about the process of writing a book while at the same time helping the profile of our business.

A good way to test the purpose of your book is to talk to a few people.

Have a look online, in bookstores and libraries. Are there already a lot of books like the one you are writing? If there is, is there a different angle you can take that will make it different to the others already on the market?

Identify your readership

There will be more than one market for your book. Try to identify at least two. For example, if you write a children's book the obvious reader is the child but a child won't buy the book. It will be a parent, grandparent or caregiver.

Have a think about primary and secondary markets.

The Book Book – the reader

A primary market is a person interested in writing a book

A secondary market might be a person interested in getting in to the publishing or writing field.

Specialist market: A business person wanting to write a book to convey their special skills.

Where can you find your readers?

There are many ways to find your ideal reader:

+ Online
+ Libraries/bookstores
+ Associations, government bodies
+ Specialist groups
+ Networks

This is where you can find some information that you might need, like demographics, lifestyles, size of market and geographical locations.

For example, these are the places I would go to research my readers for *The Book Book*:

+ Australian Society of Authors
+ Writing Australia
+ *Bookseller and Publisher* magazine
+ Nielsen BookScan
+ Australian Bureau of Statistics.

Besides looking online and at bookstores or libraries, you can also access government bodies and associations.

The *Directory of Australian Associations* is an expensive option but well worth it if you are planning to raise revenue from your book.

With extensive details on over 4,300 organisations and 9,500 key personnel, *Directory of Australian Associations* can put you in touch with your next market or corporate alliance. It is the most comprehensive resource available for information on every specialty interest group in the country, including the non-profit sector.

Identify at least two types of people
who will read your book.

_____

_____

_____

_____

_____

_____

_____

_____

_____

_____

_____

_____

_____

_____

_____

_____

_____

_____

_____

_____

_____

_____

Where will you find your readers?

map

The writing can start soon but first think about what you're going to do with this book.

Once you've decided what type of book you'd like to write, you need to sit down and plan it out.

Start with writing down what sort of things you'd like to include in the book.

Set down a chapter by chapter breakdown. Drawing a rough picture of it can be good too. This works for any kind of book, fiction or non-fiction.

Treat the writing of each chapter like a self-contained piece, so you don't feel overwhelmed.

Have a look in the library or a bookstore at the kind of book that you'd like to produce. Will it be a big fat tome that might be like a bible for the subject that you're writing about? Is it a handbook, is it a picture book?

The Book Book – intention

This book is intended to be a handbook of information for people wanting to write and publish their book. Writing a book is hard work but if approached in the right way, can be an enjoyable and rewarding experience.

The Book Book started with a plan like this:

+ A slim paperback with 160 pages, pocket-size format.
+ I wrote out the main points that I wanted to talk about and could see that the book could be divided into twelve parts.
+ In this way, the book could be written in chunks and didn't seem like a huge task.

Most books are structured in the same way in terms of content, regardless of what kind they are. A fiction novel might not have a lot of the end matter.

When you look at other books you will notice these sections:

Half title page
Title page
Imprint page
    Contents
    Foreword
    Preface
    Acknowledgement
    Dedication
        Body
        Main Text in chapters
        or parts
            End matter
            Epilogue
            Afterword
            About the author
            Glossary
            Bibliography
            Index
            Marketing material

Start mapping out your book. Jot down what elements you want to include.

Will you include images? If so, what might they be of?

_____

_____

_____

_____

_____

_____

_____

_____

_____

_____

_____

_____

_____

_____

_____

_____

_____

_____

_____

_____

_____

_____

Draw your book in a series of pictures. This works regardless of the type of book you're writing. Don't worry if you can't draw well.

The Book Book – the map

I had a rough idea of what I wanted to include in the book. My biggest problem was to decide what to leave out so that it didn't become a huge book with so much information to wade through, causing you to become overwhelmed and wondering if writing a book is just too much work.

It was simply a matter of mapping out how the structure of the book might go. This was fairly easy because I already know the important steps needed to publish a book. And so the twelve chapters that are included are what I consider the twelve most important aspects of creating a successful book.

Once I had those twelve features mapped out, it was a matter of then filling in the important aspects to each of those.

write

I bet you didn't know that there was so much to do before you got to the actual writing. You could start writing without all of that preparation but I can assure you that you will end up creating a messy manuscript and it will end up being more work than necessary.

By now you have a plan of how your book might look. This may change as you start writing so don't stress about that. At least you have a starting point. When I first started planning *The Book Book*, I decided that it should be in five parts but that soon changed when I began to work on it. It didn't matter too much because I simply broke up the parts in to appropriate chapters.

Depending on what you are writing about, the actual writing may or may not come easily. I suggest that you take a short writing course or some workshops to get you in the right frame of mind. Better yet, join a writing group. By hanging out with other writers you will gain confidence and experience in your writing. Other writers are the best people to show your work to for constructive criticism.

Most cities have a writers' centre that has great information about writing workshops, mentorships and competitions.

Write regularly. Every day if possible. This way you will gain momentum with your project and you will find that you are thinking about it every day, even when you're in the shower, or driving. That means that when you sit down at your desk to continue, you'll keep the flow going. If you don't make writing a habit, every time you sit down you'll find that you'll spend a good deal of time rereading your work and trying to get back into a rhythm.

How much writing constitutes a book?

It does depend on what kind of book it is but generally you could aim for at least 40,000 words for a non-fiction book. A fiction novel is generally around 80,000 words. A teen novel around 50,000 but a kid's picture book under 400 words.

A word on children's books. You might read the above and say, '400 words! I'll write a children's book. How hard can it be?' While the children's book market is very strong it's also very competitive. Let's just say that a picture book can take years to create and those 400 words are painstakingly worked at over and over again.

As you're writing the first draft of your book, don't get too bogged down by the quality. Try to just tell the story you want to tell, keep the momentum going and get a rough draft finished.

You could do this quite quickly if you worked on it every day and sat down to write it in sections. For instance, when I sit down and providing I'm in a good groove, I could write about 1000 words in one hour. That means that I could write my 40,000 words in about 40 hours (give or take). Of course it's very exhausting mentally to write that solidly in a week but maybe you could do it over a month. To break it down, you could aim to write 1000 words per day, five days per week. That would take about eight weeks to complete. It all depends on your workload and the aim for your project.

Where to start

I could actually write another whole book on the craft of writing but since that isn't my intention for this book, I will outline a few hints to help you get started.

A good writing space away from distractions is essential. Procrastination will be your enemy.

Read other books on your subject or in the style that you like to get inspired and to learn your craft. I don't mean that you should copy other people's work but learn from it.

There is no perfect formula for a book. Each story has something unique to share (if not, don't write it!). If you are writing a business book and aim for 40,000 words but you find yourself waffling after about 30,000, then that's all you should write. Please don't try to fill space just for the sake of it. You'll just annoy your reader who is investing hours with you.

What makes good writing?

Write about what you know. Be you. This is fairly obvious, isn't it? You wouldn't write a how-to book on horse riding if you've never done it. Of course you can go and learn about it and gain experience and knowledge that you can then pass on to your reader. If you're writing a novel about fifteenth-century France, you can't just make it up even though your story might be made up. You need to do a lot of reading and learn about the details that you might use in your story. You can be sure that if you have details wrong that you'll have readers give you negative feedback about your book. There's always at least one reader who knows that that type of garment would NOT have been worn by a person in fifteenth century France.

Everybody has a **voice** and this comes out when they write. However, some writers try very hard to write in such a way as to be unnatural to them and it really shows in the writing. Don't try to use language that isn't natural to you.

Use **active** rather than passive voice. Construct sentences where the subject 'acts'. For example (the dog is the subject),

1. The dog bit the boy – is *active*
2. The boy was bitten by the dog – is *passive*.

This brings your sentences to life!

Your sentences need to have light and shade – **passion** – and to make the reader want to continue on. Who wants to read a biography that is a blow by blow timeline of a person's life? The reader wants descriptive language that draws them into the story and makes them care and believe what you are telling them.

Use **layman's** terms rather than jargon. I could easily write this book using writing and publishing terms that the person off the street has no idea about. Of course the reader can go and look words up on Google or ask someone but there's only so much a reader will put up with. That means that your writing needs to be accessible to anyone who might pick up your book, regardless of their knowledge. If you are writing an academic book aimed at people in a very specific industry, then terminology relevant to the readership is fine.

Avoid **cliché**. The next time you read the paper or a book, take note of the clichés that will be everywhere. Quite often they are used so much that we don't even notice them. We even use them in everyday conversation and of course there is no writing police who will come tapping you on your shoulder but if you want interesting, engaging writing, try to avoid cliché as much as possible, or at least minimise it.

Layout is important. Start a new paragraph when you begin talking about a new idea. This helps the reader navigate your story. The same goes if you have dialogue. When a new person starts to speak, start a new line.

The **tone** you use should fit the type of book you're writing. For instance, this book is casual. It feels like I might be talking to you. Because of this I chose not to use a formal or academic writing style.

Use stories or describe situations to show your reader what you mean. This will help them to relate to you and your story. **Anecdotes** or **case**

studies are very useful. Make sure that these anecdotes are actually relevant to the story and not just some funny little aside. They are useful to illustrate a point.

From now on, when you read, you will notice the length of sentences. The length of a sentence and the types of words you use will change the way the story is read. For instance, short sentences will make the **pace** snappy. If you're writing a thriller, you might find yourself writing shorter sentences when the drama is high because it helps to create that fast pace as if someone is running from danger. Or if you are writing about something very technical, you might like to use shorter sentences so that the information is easier to follow.

Every story is better with the use of **humour**. Funny anecdotes or situations that illustrate your point will be more memorable. Think about this. When a group of people stand around at the pub swapping stories, invariably the funny ones get the most reaction.

Use the **senses**. Funnily enough, reading is a sensory thing. I think this is why many people love a 'real' printed book because it adds to the experience. When you're describing something, think about different ways to describe it to add interest to your story. For example, instead of describing a cold day, say it is grey or that your ears hurt from the cold.

The **structure** is important so that your reader doesn't get confused:

+ **Beginning** – introduce the subject and get straight to the point.
+ **Middle** – deal with your points in a logical order and stick to the topic and
+ **End** – round off your story by bringing it back to the beginning.

Ideally, your opening sentence should be shorter than what follows and should attempt to hook your reader immediately.

The first draft of your book is about putting flesh onto the bones that you created when you mapped out your book. Because of this, the first draft should be written continuously and as fast as possible according to your other commitments. This will give you more likelihood of getting out a full story no matter what the quality is like. Once you have this first draft, you can revise it in bits and pieces. The first draft will be full of mistakes and holes so I advise you to NOT show this draft to anyone until you have revised it.

If you're struggling to sit down to write your story, why not try dictating it? There are many great Apps available, like Dragon dictation for the iPhone, where you can talk into your microphone and the text will appear on the screen. It may need a bit of cleaning up but is quite fast compared with typing. There are services that you can use that will use your dictated file and type it into a document.

5

rewrite

So what do you do once you have a first draft? Is it pure gold? There are many would-be writers out there who think that once they've written this draft that they have written a book and it's ready to be sent to a publisher for consideration. This manuscript is a long way off being ready to be shown the light of day, no matter how good a writer you are. Be ready to rewrite it many times.

It's now time to make it into gold. This is where you need to get very picky about every word that will go into your book. If you're unsure if it makes sense or if the structure works, you could pay an independent reader or editor to read it and write you a report. This is called a manuscript assessment and can be very valuable to test the strength of your book. In an assessment, you will be given a report that goes through the manuscript in detail and reports back to you on the quality of your writing, the grammar, the structure, credibility, characters (if a novel), attention to detail, whether it fits your readership and any other things you might like highlighted.

If you don't want an assessment, get your peers or trusted writing friends to read it and give you feedback. Please don't ask friends or family to do this (unless they are qualified) because they won't be able to give you valuable feedback except to say it's good or bad or something unproductive like that.

Once you have your feedback, decide what changes you might make that you agree with. You will find that you will go over the book a few times before it is ready to edit. Don't rush this process. Sometimes, when you've worked on something with intensity, you start to get very close to the work and will find that you cannot look at it objectively. Quite often you will totally miss mistakes because you have read over and over it to the point that the words become white noise. This is also why an author should not proofread their own work. It's always better to get someone who hasn't seen it before to read it over.

Once you feel that the manuscript is as good as you can make it, it's time for a line by line edit (copyedit).

'But I've already reworked it ten times!' I hear you moan.

All that reworking is draining but necessary to iron out any problems with your story. The line by line edit is to make sure that the manuscript is clean and ready to be shown to the wider world.

Less IS more. Write your story in the least possible amount of words. This doesn't mean you skimp on details. Be succinct but thorough.

A good exercise is to look at each

sentence and ask yourself if it is relevant to the story. If you can take it out and it doesn't affect the story, then do so.

Reading your work out loud is a very good process. You will 'hear' the problems with it and stumble over awkward words and phrases. Be prepared to read over your book several times. You will get sick of it, bit I promise you will end up with a better product.

Here are the kind of things that an editor will look for when editing a book:

+ Is the whole book written in the same tense?
+ Is the language clear and understandable?
+ Is there repetition?
+ Is it succinct?
+ Are all the details included to give the reader the full picture?
+ Are there irrelevant details?
+ Is punctuation and grammar correct?
+ Is there an overuse of specific terms such as 'however', 'but',

- 'so', 'maybe'?
- ✦ Is it full of clichés?
- ✦ Is information copied from external sources such as the internet, or other books?
- ✦ Has permission been sought to use any copied information (text or images)?
- ✦ Is the book engaging?

A note on copyright

When a person creates something they automatically own the copyright. It doesn't need to be registered, so long as you can prove that you are the creator.

Respect other peoples' copyright. Going onto Google, looking up information and cutting and pasting information is ILLEGAL. Same goes for the use of images. So, if you are using information that is not your own, please seek permission.

What next?

Once you feel that the book is as good as you can make it, leave it for a week or two, then read it once more from start to finsh as if you are a potential reader. This space away from it will allow you to detach a little and see it with fresh eyes and ears.

If you plan on engaging an editor, this is the time to hand it over. Or, if you feel that it's ready, you can hand it over to your book designer.

publish

Once you've written your book, what do you do now? We live in exciting times because there are many options open to a writer in terms of getting work out into the world. It isn't up to a big publisher to say *yes* or *no* to your work anymore.

In the past many people scoffed at the idea of self-publishing, saying that it was vain, but these days it is so easy and affordable that I ask, *Why wouldn't you?*

Virginia Woolf and her husband published their own work from their kitchen table, thus founding *Hogarth Press*. They believed in their work and didn't see the need to wait for some big publisher to beckon them in and tell them that they were geniuses.

Other authors include, Mark Twain, *Huckleberry Finn*; John Grisham, *A Time to Kill* (his first book was sold from the boot of his car); Jack Canfield and Mark Hansen, *Chicken Soup for the Soul*; Beatrix Potter, *Peter Rabbit* series; Gertrude Stein; Margaret Atwood; DH Lawrence; and George Bernard Shaw. There are many more but you get the point.

Traditional mainstream publishing

Traditionally, authors had little option to get published unless they sent their work to a mainstream publisher. This is where you send your manuscript to them, and wait up to nine months for an answer. To top it off, publishing etiquette deems that you only send it to one publisher at a time! The waiting can be excruciating. It can also feel like you are wasting valuable time. That's okay if you have a 'real' job and this is something you want to do on the side and time isn't a big issue. But if you're a business person and you'd like a book to enhance your profile, you might find that time is of the essence. If you've written a novel and it's taken you years to write (not at all uncommon), you might be happy to wait.

It's not unheard of that a writer has submitted their work to a mainstream publisher and gotten a book deal very quickly. Not unheard of but also not common. About three percent of books sent to traditional publishers will land a publishing deal.

Publishing process

The normal process for traditional publishing goes like this:

1. Prepare your manuscript by looking at the guidelines from the publisher. This may include a biography, a synopsis of the book and one to three chapters of the book.
2. Submit your work to the publisher's slush pile.
3. Wait

4. Wait
5. Wait
6. Wait
7. You will receive a letter to say they are rejecting or accepting it, or that they may want to talk further with you about it.
8. If you're rejected, you can send it to another publisher and repeat the process.
9. If you're accepted, they will assign an editor to you once you've signed a contract.
10. The contract will state that you, the author, will receive between 7.5–10% royalty on the retail price of the book. This is about two dollars for every book depending on the retail price. Ebooks are usually 50% commission.

The manuscript will be edited and you will rework it in consultation with your editor and your publisher.

1. While you're working on the manuscript, the art department will start

designing the cover and marketing material. You may have some say in the look of the cover.

2. Your manuscript will be typeset, your book printed.

3. Your book will be launched.

4. Depending on the size of the publishing company, there will be publicity organised and you will be expected to appear at bookstores and libraries to spruik your book. You won't get paid for these appearances. Small publishers generally have very little marketing budget.

5. The publishing company will organise your book to be distributed to bookstores where sales will happen.

6. With some luck you will receive some commission from your book. With a lot of luck you may have a bestseller and make a name for yourself. Having a great book that is

marketed well will help you but sometimes it's simply a matter of being in the right place at the right time.

There are many pluses to being published by a mainstream publisher. There is no risk on your part and you don't need any money. A publisher knows what they are doing and also has a large publicity base to use that you may not be able to afford.

The Book Book – options

This part was obviously easy for me because I knew that I would publish it myself. For many of my clients I do encourage them to think about both options – traditional publishing and self-publishing – for any project. I quite often suggest that an author try the traditional path first and if nothing happens or it's taking too long they have the option to do it themselves. Either way, make the book as polished as possible to give it the best chance of succeeding.

Self-publishing

Self-publishing is a great way to realise your dream of becoming an author in less time, while having full control of your project. You will of course need to invest some money into the project for editing, design, layout and printing but if you do your homework, you should be able to make your money back very quickly.

Printing

You can search for a printer and print a print run of your choice. Any print run under 1000 copies will be digitally printed. This is slightly more expensive per unit than offset printing but I wouldn't advise large print runs initially. You're better off getting a small run and then reprinting once you know how the book is going. This of course depends on what your intention is for your book. If you're producing something as a give away at a fair or to clients and actually need thousands of copies, then by all means get what you need.

Print on Demand (POD) is another great way to print without forking out money for printing. It requires that the purchaser actually pays for the printing when they buy the book. This means that if they buy it online, some of the purchase price will go to the POD company, some will go to you and some to the seller. Each book is then printed as it is purchased and therefore requires no storage facility or outlay of money. Of course the unit price for each book will be higher and your profit lower. Some reputable companies include Blurb, Lulu, and Lightning source.

If you're only wanting to publish an ebook, you can do this directly with Amazon, who will then sell the book online for you. Or you can search for a reputable business that can convert your files to the correct format for various eReaders.

If you decide that you will go down the self-publishing path, here are the next steps required.

Publishing timeline

The process to self-publishing is very similar to mainstream publishing but it's a good idea to draw up a timeline so that you have the big picture in your head. The chapters in this book are meant to be a guide to this timeline but here are the basic steps. They are the same whether you publish a printed book or an ebook.

1. write book
2. edit
3. design cover (the earlier the better)
4. layout book
5. proofread book
6. send to printer (or create ebook)
7. implement marketing plan
8. launch book
9. sell it
10. maximise your opportunites.

Here is your opportunity to plan out your publishing project.

design

If you've decided to self-publish, you will need to think about the design of your book. This doesn't mean that you will actually need to do the physical design but you will need to have some ideas that you can discuss with your book designer.

Format

The format of your book will make a big difference to the price per unit. Go and pick up a handful of books from your own bookshelf and measure the sizes. You'll begin to see the common sizes. Better yet, buy a copy of a book that you like the look of (or borrow from the library) and measure it and study the elements that appeal to you.

The following formats are the most common in the industry:

+ A format 181mm x 111mm
+ B format 198mm x 128mm
+ B+ format 210mm x 135mm
+ Demy format 216mm 135mm
+ A5 format 210mm x 148mm
+ C format 234mm x 153mm
+ C+ format 234mm x 180mm
+ B5 format 250mm x 205mm
+ Sub A4 format 290mm x 205mm
+ A4 format 297mm x 210mm.

All of these standard formats can be printed digitally. Check with your printer about offset options. Of course, there are many other options for sizes but choosing a standard size is more efficient and economical.

Paper stock

The type of paper to use in your book is the next thing to think about. Again, it depends on your book. The whiteness and the thickness are essential to the look and feel of your book. If it's a novel or business book, the choices aren't so essential but if it's a coffee table book or has images in it, you do need to choose more carefully. I suggest you talk to a printer. I find that printers are a wonderful breed. I've never come across more helpful and patient people in any industry and I can assure you that I have and still do ask what must be stupid questions.

Here are some common types of paperstock:

White offset

This paper is a brilliant white and offers good opacity and bulk. This premium offset paper is good for high standard text and image reproduction.

Book cream

This is used often for novels and is a creamy shade with an even quality and shade with high bulk and opacity, which contributes to superior readability.

Bulky white

A white mechanical stock that is

ideal for use when bulk and opacity are critical to the finished book.

Please note that papers have different weights that are measured as grams per square metre (gsm). Think about your standard copy paper that you use for your printer. It will usually be 80gsm.

Register your book

There are no laws to say that you need to register a book that you publish but even if you don't intend to sell your book commercially, it's worthwhile registering your book and obtaining a 13-digit International Standard Book Number (ISBN). Every book that has an ISBN is stored at the National Library in Canberra, as well as the library in the state that it was published in. You could say that that way your book is recorded for prosterity if nothing else. If you do plan to sell it, booksellers and distributors will more than likely not take it on without an ISBN.

Thorpe-Bowker   manages   the

allocation of an ISBN. The website is at the back of this book.

Alternatively, many printers or publishing businesses (like ours) can organise an ISBN for you.

Take a look at one of those books on your shelf and you'll see that the ISBN is on the back cover, along with a barcode. It's also advisable to obtain a barcode to make life easier for the bookseller to stock it on their bookshelves. The barcode also records the number of sales an ISBN makes and this is recorded by BookScan. This is how books make it on to the top ten lists, through this measuring system. This is the aim: to make everything very easy for the bookseller to deal with it.

Design

Everyone judges a book by its cover. Here are some tips to consider for your cover:

+ If using dark colours, go for a glossy lamination to avoid scuff marks.

- Wrap your colour/image from the front cover and around the spine. This will avoid misalignment in the binding process.
- Set images such as logo and barcode at least 5mm inside the cover edge to allow for trimming.
- Consider a laminate to protect the cover of your book.
- Spines of less than 5mm should not have any type.
- Double-check your ISBN and barcode numbers match.

Front cover

Try to imagine your book on a bookshelf in a bookstore or on Amazon. There are thousands of other books shelved around it, so you need to give your book every possible chance of standing out from the crowd. The look and feel of your cover should also reflect the reader that you want to attract. There's no point having lovely floral fonts and pastel colours if you want to attract

a young, reader. If you don't feel
confident designing a cover yourself
have a book designer help you.

Back cover

The blurb is very important too. When
a potential reader picks up your
book, the cover will be what attracts
them. Then they'll turn it over to see
what the book is about. You have
mere seconds to hook a reader. You
must engage them very quickly. If
you have a way of obtaining a quote
or testimonial about you or your
book, from someone well-known, this
will go a long way to enhancing your
credibility.

Spine

The spine only needs the title and
your name but it must be very easy
to read. Very few physical books
are displayed face out, so the spine
may be the first thing that a browser
sees.

Binding

There are many ways to bind a book

but you'll soon realise that the choice is obvious. A novel or non-fiction book is usually perfect or burst bound. That creates a flat edge, with all the pages bound by a special glue, then attached to the cover. Small books or books that have a small budget might have a saddle stitch or staple binding. Workbooks, notebooks and diaries tend to be spiral bound.

The text

There are a few things to consider for the internals of your book. You can squeeze as much into each page in order to make the book more compact and save money on printing or you can give some thought to the design and make it a visually pleasing object.

Your book designer (or you) can try out a few different options with the layout. It should reflect the type of book it is. Looking at books on your bookshelf is a good way to get ideas. Here are some things to think about:

- ✦ Type of font and size (an older audience will appreciate large font, teens will like something trendy).
- ✦ The white space or width of margins.
- ✦ The heading styles.
- ✦ Will you have a running header?
- ✦ Will page numbers be centred or on the outside of the margins?
- ✦ The formatting of tables.
- ✦ How images (if any) will be treated (with captions or other design elements).

Printing

There are many, many really good printers in Australia. Every single one that I have dealt with has been efficient, friendly and patient, as well as punctual. It's worth asking for at least three quotes from three different printers and talking to them about your options. For instance, the type of paper you use will make the spine fatter. Little clues like that are helpful.

The amount of copies you need to get printed is also very important. That will depend on your budget and your intention for your book.

You also need to check in with your printer ahead of time to make sure that they can print your books for the date that you require them. Make sure you allow for printing time in your publishing schedule. There's nothing worse than setting your launch date but not having books there on the day.

Ebooks

There are also many ways to produce an ebook. You may decide to produce a print book in conjunction with an ebook, or just an ebook. There are companies that will create an ebook for you and sell it online. You will need a separate ISBN for your ebook. The following companies are some that can sell your ebook for you.

+ Smashwords
+ Amazon
+ Apple iBook

There are many different file types but these are common ones:

+ Pdf
+ Epub
+ Mobi

Promotional material

While you are designing the book and cover, you should also think about any promotional material you might need. Bookmarks, postcards, flyers and posters are all good ways to promote a book.

market

The marketing of your book is as important as the content and design. Without marketing your book, you will have great difficulty selling it. This might not matter if you're publishing it as a giveaway but most people would at least like to make their investment back in sales.

Marketing your book will depend on the purpose of it, your time and the amount of money you can spend on promotion.

There are three steps to marketing your book:

1. Identify the people who will read your book.
2. Create a marketing plan that includes a timeline and budget.

3. Employ your marketing plan.

How to connect with your readers

As part of your marketing plan, think about who you will target. Your call to action will be the first thing to think about when creating some promotional material. A call to action is the words that urge a person in a sales promotion message to take immediate action, such as *Act Now*, *Call Now*, *Buy Now* or *Click Here*.

The following list might be places that you can connect with your reader and deliver your call to action:

+ Your networks
+ Specialist groups
+ Free publicity
+ Paid advertising
+ Self-promotion, social media, author talks
+ Website
+ Book trailer

Your networks

Action: create a list of people who you think might be great advocates to pass on information about your book.

This is fairly self-explanatory. Using your networks is all about talking to people and getting them to pass on the information by word-of-mouth.

Specialist groups

Action: create a list of specialist groups that suit your book.

When you were online researching these groups, you will have created a list of relevant groups for your book. Use this list as your mailing list when sending out promotional material. Think about what you can do for them and offer free talks and author signings at meetings. Or offer to write a free article for a newsletter in exchange for self-promotion.

Free publicity

Action: Create a media list that will suit your book.

Start by looking at your local paper. Think about a hook that could be a potential article in the paper that might help promote you and your book. Local papers are especially interested in local personalities or current trends. Or maybe your book has a topic that relates to something that is happening in the community like 'How to keep chooks'. The local paper might review books or could write an article about your book. Create a media release to send to these outlets.

The local radio station might have a community events timeslot where you can talk about a topic (that might be your expertise). Offer to come in to talk about it and offer a book as a give away to the listeners.

Paid advertising

Action: create a list of places that would reach your target audience.

Advertising is very expensive so you need to make sure that your dollars are used wisely. It's silly to advertise in a fashion magazine if your reader is a business magnate.

Create a schedule for any paid advertising because some print materials require a long lead-time for advertising.

Self-promotion

Action: create a list of possible ways to tell the world about you and your book. There are many, many ways to spread the word through social media, your website, author talks and libraries.

Create a Facebook page for yourself or your book. This is a great way to start building a fanbase for your project.

A website

It does depend on how much money you have to invest in your project but a personalised website is a great idea. There are plenty of free ways to create a website now, using companies like WordPress. You can set up a dedicated website for your book or yourself. Keep it simple with just a few pages. A blog is a great way to connect with readers. You'll also need to set up a page to sell the book and then maybe another page that tells readers about you.

Book trailer

A book trailer is like an advertisement that gives readers a taste of what your book is about. It doesn't have to be a big budget event and it shouldn't be too long. Think about TV advertisements. They are usually about 30 seconds long. Plan your book trailer to be between 30–90 seconds for great impact. Your trailer can go up onto YouTube and can be cross-linked to your website, Facebook and other online sources.

Do you have the time to market your book?

The amount of time you have available to promote your book, the better it will sell. Again, the purpose of your book will determine how you will market it. If you are a business coach and have written a book about your expertise, your book can become part of your sales kit. You can offer it as part of mentoring sessions or as giveaways to entice people to use you as a coach.

How will you get your books into the readers' hands?

We live in a fast-paced world and there are many different ways for consumers to purchase your book.

+ Will you go door-to-door of every book shop?
+ Will you engage a distributor?
+ Will you sell online, on your website or via Amazon?
+ Other websites?
+ Conferences
+ Other.

Book launch(es)

The book launch should be part of your marketing timeline. This is the chance to celebrate all of your hard work, show friends, family and colleagues your book and sell a bulk amount of books in one go to off-set your investment.

Engage a specialist

There are people who specialise in book publicity. The ideal scenario for a book publicist is a three month program that works on pre-release publicity. The publicity might start a month before the book comes out and follows through on its release. A publicist will have connections to all the right media to suit your book and should be able to get you in print media, on TV and radio.

Ideally you should aim to have the book printed a month before it comes out officially so that the publicist can start sending out copies for review.

The Book Book – marketing plan

This book is a product for Busybird Publishing and will be part of our business marketing, therefore it doesn't need a concentrated marketing plan. In fact, it's part of our bigger business marketing plan.

Marketing plan

Now that we've touched on ways and places to market your book, it's time for you to get down to work and make your plan.

A good way to start is to set a launch date off in the future and work backwards from there.

In mainstream publishing, the usual production time is about eighteen months but when you self-publish it can be done in about three months if you work hard.

Who is your ideal reader?

Your book title:

The format:

The price (RRP):

The genre:

List some similar books:

How is yours different?

Your goals for the book?

Income (put a $ amount):

To increase your profile?

To become famous?

How many books will you print?

How many will you give away?

Action	Date
Finish first draft	
Rewrite book	
Edit manuscript	
Send manuscript to publisher	
Or start self-publishing	
Design cover	
Design internals	
Have book typeset	
Proofread book	
Create promotional material	
Promote launch	
Implement marketing plan	
Send book to printer (allow 2–3 weeks)	
Send out media releases	
Start pre-selling books	
Have launch	
Enjoy the ride!	

polish

You can now see your book project coming together and you know what will unfold once you have the book in your hands. It's important, though, to implement your marketing plan early so that you are well on your way to selling copies before it has arrived.

By now you've written and edited your book and you and your designer have worked out the 'look and feel' for it. At this stage, you need to tie up all the loose ends and make sure you are ready to fly once the book is released.

Before you send that book off to the printer, make sure that you have it thoroughly checked over. Proofreading is very important. You don't want to have spent all this time writing, editing and designing only to have the book come out with a glaring mistake in it. It isn't a total disaster if you do but you don't want to have wasted money on printing. That's the beauty of digital printing. You can get a small print run to begin with, so you won't have such an outlay of money.

So what do you need to look for in the proofreading stage? This is where you check for spelling mistakes, typos, layout issues and design. It isn't the time to correct any editing problems because they should've been done before the designer sets up the layout. It is advisable that you check a hardcopy of your book because you will miss twenty-five per cent of errors on screen.

Here are some common things to look for:

The cover

+ Check that the ISBN on the imprint page is the same as on the back cover.

- ✦ Is the spine width correct as per printers specifications?
- ✦ Are all elements of the cover design within 5mm of the trim edge of the cover?
- ✦ Check spelling of names and titles.
- ✦ Check the blurb for errors and formatting.

The internals

- ✦ Check that the page numbers are sequential.
- ✦ If there are running headers, make sure they are correct and match the chapter heading.
- ✦ Check the contents page numbers match the actual pages.
- ✦ Go through each line to correct spelling errors and typos.
- ✦ Make sure there are no lines missing. This can happen when the pages run-on.
- ✦ New chapters usually start on the right side unless you have chosen otherwise.
- ✦ If there are images, are they positioned correctly and are the

captions correct?

+ There should be no running headers on chapter title pages.
+ Check for consistent font and sizing.
+ Look for errors in the layout, such as margins, spaces between paragraphs, and spaces between words.
+ Are the images in the correct position and captioned correctly?

Once you feel happy with your proofreading, have the corrections made and then check it again because sometimes new errors can be introduced.

It's now time to send your book to the printer. Congratulations!

Depending on the turnaround time for the printer, you will now wait impatiently for the book to come back. By now, you hopefully have been spreading the word about your upcoming book and maybe even have some preorders.

If you sell out quickly of your

first print run, don't worry. Printers always keep a file copy of your book onsite. This means that you can request further books without re-supplying the files. But if you want to make changes to the book, you will need to supply new files.

For any changes to the book, or a different format, you need to apply for a new ISBN.

launch

The launch is a very important step for your book. Please don't skip it. There are a few reasons for this. First of all, it's a celebration of all the hard work to this point, one that you can share with family, friends and colleagues.

Next, it's the first point of contact with potential readers. Sure, some of them will be family or friends who might only be buying it to support you but each of those people have their own network of contacts. Word can spread.

Also, a launch will give you an initial burst of income from sales which will help you recoup some of your expenses.

Here are some things to consider

for your launch:

+ When
+ Where
+ Who to invite
+ Costs
+ Publicity for launch
+ Marketing materials for launch – posters, flyers, banner, bookmarks, postcards, invitations
+ How many books needed for launch
+ Who will sell books (you will be too busy)?
+ Will you have entertainment?
+ What food/drinks will you provide?
+ Will you photograph/film the event?

The location will depend on the type of book you have and who your readership is. For example, if you have written a gardening book, you might hold the launch at a nursery. If you've written a children's book you could launch at a library or bookshop. There are many variations but you could think outside the square a little and have fun with it. Treat it like a party.

The attendee (or target audience) might determine the time of the launch. The gardening book might be for older people so afternoon tea will be appropriate. A children's book might be mid-morning.

Invite as many people as you can. The more the better. If your budget is small, get people to bring a plate or hold it at a cafe where they buy their own coffee and cake. You can keep the cost down by keeping the refreshments simple, like tea and coffee and cake.

The launch running sheet

If you haven't been to a launch before, here is a typical running schedule:

1. Set up room for guests (allow a table for food, one for books, space for signing).
2. Guests arrive.
3. Guests mingle.
4. Welcome guests officially.

5. MC introduces guest speaker/launcher (this might be someone well known in the field related to the book or someone of note or just a good friend).
6. Launcher speaks about book and author and officially launches the book.
7. Author talks about the book.
8. Guests buy book.
9. Author signs books.
10. Guests mingle and chat to author.
11. Clean up.

sell

If you've been lucky enough to be picked up by a publisher, you don't have to worry so much about the selling aspect of it. But don't think for one minute that you can sit back and enjoy the commission coming in. These days, publishers don't put as much money into marketing and gone are the days when a book can sell well if you are a hermit. People aren't so interested in the tortured writer persona anymore.

You will be asked by the publisher to do a book tour where you will be expected to go to bookshops and libraries, talk about the book and sign copies. You won't get paid for this time but it will pay off in sales of your book.

Selling your book

I won't beat around the bush. Selling your book is the hardest part about the whole process. This is also dependant on what your purpose for writing is. If selling your book isn't your top priority, then it doesn't matter.

Financials

There are some things to consider when selling your book in terms of bookkeeping:

+ Do you need an ABN?
+ Are you already a business entity?
+ Do you need to be registered for GST?
+ How will you manage the accounting?

If you are already in business, consider these things:

+ Do you own the rights to the book, or does your business?
+ Will you keep it separate to your business?

What are the implications to your business in terms of:

+ Legal requirements
+ Financials
+ Marketing
+ How much of your time will the book take away from your business?
+ How best to use your book to enhance your business.

Where can you sell it?

Bookstores, gift shops, Amazon or other online book stores, or from your car boot are the main places that you could sell your book.

You can get your book into bookstores by contacting them yourself or using a distributor. A distributor will charge you 18% commision (of RRP) and take it across the nation to all of their contacts. A bookstore will then take a further 40% commission. These are standard costs.

Usually a bookstore takes the book on consignment. This means that you won't get paid for it until it is sold. If it doesn't get sold, it will be returned to you.

If you plan to sell it online, you can do it via Amazon or your own website. Amazon isn't the only place to sell but it is the biggest and most well known. It's also very easy to set up an account on Amazon and follow the instructions to sell either your printed book or ebook.

If you're selling from your website, you can set up a PayPal (or similar) account to make it easy for people to buy your book by clicking on a *Buy Now* option. This is very easy to set up from a PayPal account and you can direct the money to a nominated account. Don't forget that, for accounting purposes, you need to factor in GST if you are registered.

If you're selling the book yourself, you will need to take into account postage costs. These you can add to the book price. You will also have to handle the packaging and postage unless you have someone who can do it for you.

If you've opted for POD, all the postage and handling will be taken care of by the POD company. Costs will be taken out of the sale and profits given back to you. POD costs vary, so talk to your provider. Many printers offer a POD service.

maximise

You now have your book in your hands and you've presented it to the world. It may or may not take off straight away. There will be an initial flurry of interest but this will slow down unless you keep up the momentum.

Speaking opportunities

It doesn't matter what type of book you've written. There will be ways that you can maximise it and keep spreading the word about your story. Look for any opportunity to speak to an audience about your book.

Libraries

Don't underestimate the value of the library. You can market your book by offering a free 'Meet the Author' session in exchange for selling the book. Libraries are changing and are no longer the place where you must be quiet. They are very much community hubs and have great spaces to share ideas.

You can offer similar scenarios to the following groups that fit your subject matter:

+ Associations
+ Specialist groups
+ Conferences
+ Launches
+ Chamber of Commerce meetings
+ Network meetings

Online marketing plan

Create an outline of your options and a timeline that runs in line with the publishing and sale of your book at these outlets:

+ Website
+ Facebook
+ LinkedIn
+ Twitter

- Blog
- Google
- YouTube
- Webinars

Spread the word

The more you do to tell the world about your book, the better chance it'll have of being seen.

Carry a book with you at all times so that if you happen to bring it up in conversation you can show people. Most people are curious to see what you've done and will be more than happy to take a look. It doesn't mean that they'll buy it but they may tell someone else. Word of mouth is very powerful.

Use YouTube to your advantage. You can do things like film yourself reading the book, or other people reading it. Or you could talk about the book (why you did it and what it's about). Then upload the footage onto YouTube. Make sure that you crosslink with Facebook and your website if you're using them.

*Be prepared for opportunites
to open up that you never
thought possible.*

I promise you they will!

USEFUL TERMINOLOGY

Appendices Supplementary material at the end of a book usually of an explanatory nature.

Barcode A grid of black lines on the back of a book used to scan book details. It includes the ISBN.

Bibliography An organised listing of books that might have been used as references or are recommended reading.

Blurb The text on the back cover of the book. It could be a synopsis of what the book is about, a call to action or a teaser.

Book design Concept created for the look and feel of a book to appeal to target audience.

Book layout Typesetting of book with margins, page numbers, headings and images for printing.

Burst binding Flat edge spine similar to perfect binding but more durable.

Cliché As an expression which has become overused to the point of losing its original meaning, or effect, to the point of being trite or irritating, especially when at some earlier time it was considered meaningful or novel.

Copyedit An edit that goes through the whole manuscript (the copy) to check for grammar issues, spelling errors and typos line by line.

Copyright A form of intellectual property (as patents, trademarks and trade secrets are), applicable to any expressible form of an idea or information that is substantive and discrete.

CiP Cataloguing in Publication record is a bibliographic record prepared by the Library of Congress for a book that has not yet been published. Useful for libraries and bookshops to find a book before it has been released and to order it ahead of time.

Dedication A mark of affection or regard for a person that might have been inspirational or deserves credit for something.

Digital printing The use of digital technology to print. Ideal for small print runs.

Distributor A person or company that will implement a distribution service to get a book into retail outlets.

Dpi Dots per inch. Information within a digital file that relates to resolution. The more dpi in an image, the better the print quality.

ebook An electronic book created for reading on various electronic readers or platforms such as Kindle, Kobo, iPhone and computers. Common file types include epub, movi, pdf.

Emboss Raised or sunken image or lettering on a book cover.

End matter The beginning and end parts of the book that include title pages, imprint page, index or appendices.

Epilogue A piece of writing at the end of a work of literature, usually used to bring closure to the work.

Fiction Stories that are not true, such as a novel.

Folio A page number.

Foreword Written by someone other than the primary author of the work, it often tells of some interaction between the writer of the foreword and the book's primary author or the story the book tells.

Ghostwriter A person who will write a book for another person but not take credit for it, or own copyright.

Gloss A shiny surface of the cover.

Head The top of a book.

Index Sequential list of data contained within a book. It details, alphabetically, names, places and topics, along with corresponding pagination. This requires a specialist editor.

Imprint page The page that lists all publishing details, such as the ISBN, publisher, author and any disclaimers and copyright information.

ISBN International Standard Book Number of 13 digits.

Lamination A surface coating on the cover of a book to protect it from scratching.

Landscape The format of the book where the height is less than the width.

Line edit Editing that corrects a book line by line (same as copyedit).

Manuscript assessment A detailed

report given by a specialist (such as an editor) after having read a manuscript. This will give feedback on the quality of the book in terms of writing style, grammar, language, structure, character development (in fiction), legal issues, and readership.

Margins The white space at the edge of a page, outside the text.

Neilson BookScan The company that records book sales using the registered ISBN and barcode.

Non-fiction A story that is true or based on facts.

Offset printing Printing technology that allows for large scale printing at affordable prices. Best used for large quantities of books to allow for smaller unit prices.

PDF Portable Document Format. A file created from various platforms to create a fixed file, flat document that can usually be opened on any computer. The usual file requirement for printing a book.

Perfect binding A flat-edged binding.

Pixel An element of a digital image. The more pixels in an image, the better the printable quality.

Plagiarism The use of another author's language, ideas, or expressions, and the representation of them as one's own original work. This can be deemed as copyright infringement.

Portrait The format of a book where the height is more than the width.

Preface An introduction to a book written by the work's author.

Pre-press The status of a manuscript before it goes to print, usually created as a pdf.

Print area The area within the crop lines of the pre-press file.

Publishing The act of creating a product into a medium that can be consumed by the population.

Recto Right hand page of the book.

Resolution The amount of detail an image holds. For good quality print, an image should be a minumum of 300dpi.

Running header/footer Text that

appears at the top or bottom of a page within the margins but outside the text. The headers usually contain chapter headings and footers contain page numbers.

Run-ons Additional books printed after the first print run where no changes are made.

Saddle stitching The use of staples to bind a book.

Scan The use of scanning technology to copy an image into a computer file.

Slush pile Books submitted to publishers for consideration. In the days of hardcopies, this pile was literally the 'in-tray' on the desk of the editor or intern in charge of reading incoming books.

Spine The binding edge of a book.

Stock The type of paper used in printing.

Structural edit Editing that looks at the structure or 'big picture' of a book to make sure that the story flows and is believable. Structure is very important to the content of both fiction and non-fiction, to make sure that the ideas are comprehensive. It looks at language, consistency and content and is much more detailed than a copyedit.

Tail Bottom of the book.

Thorpe-Bowker The company that looks after registration of ISBNs.

TIFF Tagged Image File Format for exchanging bitmapped images between applications.

Trim marks Marks placed on copy to indicate trim marks after printing.

Typesetting The layout of a manuscript into what will be the printable file. This will include taking in design factors like margins, headings and images.

Verso Left hand page of the book.

USEFUL RESOURCES

Australian Society of Authors (ASA)

Suite C1.06 22–36 Mountail Street
Ultimo NSW 2007
asa@asauthors.org
T: 02 9211 1004
www.asauthors.org

Writing Australia Ltd

c/- Executive Office
National Library of Australia
Parkes Place
Parkes ACT 2600
info@writingaustralia.org.au
T: 02 6262 1506
www.writingaustralia.org.au

The Australian Writer's Marketplace (book) produced by the Queensland Writer's Centre
www.awmonline.com.au

Fellowship of Australian Writers

6 Davies Street
Brunswick VIC 3056
www.writers.asn.au

Book Distributors
Dennis Jones and Associates
Unit 1/10 Melrich Road
Bayswater Victoria 3153
Australia
T: 03 9762 9100
theoffice@dennisjones.com.au
www.dennisjones.com.au

Book Publicist
Scott Eathorne
Quikmark Media
0418 475 801
scott@quikmarkmedia.com.au
www.quikmarkmedia.com.au

Who is Busybird Publishing?

Busybird Publishing Studio Gallery is a hub for storytellers of all kinds.  Writers and artists will find inspiration and guidance here to make a project the best it can possibly be. We run workshops, create books and art as well as curate exhibitions for artists.

Blaise van Hecke is publisher at Busybird Publishing and is a writer, editor, photographer and artist. She has had short stories published in anthologies and placed second in the biennial short story competition for the Society of Women Writers (Vic) in 2007 for her story, *The Eleventh Summer.*

Kev Howlett is Studio Manager at Busybird Publishing and is an illustrator and photographer. He has spent twenty-five years in the commercial photographic industry taking photographs of everything from babies to Holden cars. Kev also spends a lot of time taking photographs on his travels and plans to create a picture book for each city of the world. Kev is the illustrator for the covers of *[untitled]*, our annual anthology of short stories, as well as illustrator for several c o m m i s s i o n e d children's books.

Les Zigomanis is our Publications Manager and Chief Editor at Busybird Publishing and has worked as a freelance editor for various publishers and authors. He is chief editor for our publication, *[untitled]* and is also a writer of incredible versatility. He's had two screenplays optioned and, in

2008, had two feature articles published in *Leader* Newspapers. He's also had articles and short stories published in various journals.

We have an **amazing** team of publishing interns who also help out with various publishing projects. We couldn't do so many fantastic books without their help.

Other titles by Busybird Publishing

[untitled] issue six
Price: $18.00
Publication Date: 19 Feb 2014
Format: Paperback (111mm x181mm, 158 pages)
Category: Fiction, various authors.

The Launch Book
Price: $10.00
Publication Date: 25 Feb 2014
Format: Paperback (111mm x181mm, 158 pages)
Category: Non-fiction, how to launch your own book by Les Zigomanis.

Printed in Australia
AUHW020527140622
364914AU00028B/64

9 780992 432508